OUR
AMERICA

GROWING UP IN THE CIVIL WAR

1861 to 1865

DUANE DAMON

Lerner Publications Company
Minneapolis

To my brother Wayne,
for all we shared during our own growing up years

A WORD ABOUT LANGUAGE
People who were slaves in America were forbidden to learn to read and write English. Limited to oral expression, slaves eventually developed a language recognized by many scholars as distinct from standard English. No written form of this slave language existed. The author has quoted primary sources in which slave language was transcribed in various ways. Quotes appear as they did in those sources.

Lerner Publications Company
A division of Lerner Publishing Group
241 First Avenue North
Minneapolis, MN 55401 U.S.A.

Website address: www.lernerbooks.com

The photographs in this book are reproduced with the permission of: © North Wind Picture Archives, pp. 5, 8, 14, 16, 18, 20, 23, 25, 32, 39 (top), 43, 52, 53, 55, 57; © Library of Congress, pp. 6, 9, 19, 28, 42, 44, 47, 56; © Brown Brothers, pp. 10, 33, 51; © The Society for the Preservation of New England Antiquities, p. 15; © Hulton I Archive, pp. 21, 27, 38, 39 (bottom), 40, 45, 50; © Bettmann/CORBIS, p. 22; © Stock Montage, p. 24, 30; © The Library Company of Pennsylvania, 26, 31, 58; © The Connecticut Historical Society, pp. 35, 37; © Tria Giovan/CORBIS, p. 41.

Cover photo: © Minnesota Historical Society/CORBIS

Library of Congress Cataloging-in-Publication Data

Damon, Duane.
    Growing up in the Civil War, 1861 to 1865 / by Duane Damon.
        p.   cm. — (Our America)
    Includes bibliographical references and index.
    Summary: Presents details of daily life of American children during the period from 1861 to 1865.
    ISBN: 0–8225–0656–4 (lib. bdg. : alk. paper)
    1. United States—History—Civil War, 1861–1865—Children—Juvenile literature. 2. United States—History—Civil War, 1861–1865—Social aspects—Juvenile literature. 3. Children—United States—Social life and customs—19th century—Juvenile literature. 4. Children—United States—Social conditions—19th century—Juvenile literature. 5. United States—History—Civil War, 1861–1865—Personal narratives—Juvenile literature. [1. United States—History—Civil War, 1861–1865. 2. United States—Social life and customs—19th century.] I. Title. II. Series.
E468.9 .D26 2003
973.7'083—dc21   2001007207

Manufactured in the United States of America
1 2 3 4 5 6 – JR – 08 07 06 05 04 03

CONTENTS

NOTE
TO
READERS

Did you ever have the itch to be a detective? Do you ever find yourself daydreaming about working as a detective the way they do in movies, on television, and in novels? Are you impressed by the way an investigator hunts down clues, interviews suspects and witnesses, and pieces it all together to get the big picture?

In a sense, historical researchers and writers do very much the same things. They are detectives of history. Only their beat isn't the streets and alleys of a big city. Instead, they dig into old books, newspapers, and magazines. They investigate clues hidden in paintings, songs, and poetry. They interview witnesses by reading their letters and diaries. They get to know their suspects by studying old photographs and drawings. All these are called primary sources.

In this book, the author used a number of these primary sources in piecing together the big picture. He scanned books and newspapers

A Northern soldier going off to war says good-bye to his family.

produced during the early 1860s. He read published diaries (accounts someone writes about the events in their lives as they happen) and memoirs (recollections of events written years after they happened). He studied photographs, paintings, and song lyrics—all to see how young people lived, talked, and thought during the Civil War period. The people who inhabit this book actually lived, played, worked, and went to school during the Civil War. Rich or poor, slave or free, male or female, they all have stories to tell us.

Do a little detective work of your own by investigating some of these primary sources. Follow your own trail of clues into the mysteries of being young during the Civil War (as it was called in the North) and the War between the States (as it was known in the South). You can learn how different young people then were from you and your friends and family. You just may be surprised to find out how much you're alike.

Chapter One

FIERY TRIALS

Above: Fort Sumter was the site of the first battle of the Civil War.

"Who can tell how we may be called to pass through the 'deep waters' and endure the fiery trials . . . of another year."

—*Lucy Rebecca Buck, eighteen, Virginia, Christmas 1861*

◆ ◆

THE FIRST HINT OF TROUBLE came to Tommy Wilson on a November afternoon in 1860. Many years later, he recalled "standing at my father's gateway in Augusta, Georgia. . . . and hearing someone pass and say that Mr. Lincoln was elected [president] and there was going to be war." Tommy was only four years old on that unforgettable day. "I remember running in to ask my father what it meant."

Inside his book-lined study, Tommy's father began to explain. In the months that followed, Tommy found out more. He learned that his father was serving as a chaplain (minister) in something called the Confederate Army. He noticed the nearly constant look of anxiety on his mother's face. He saw that his hometown, Augusta, was turning into a military camp.

The conflict would be unlike any the nation had ever known. Americans would fight Americans. Staggering numbers of lives would be lost. And when the Civil War was over, the United States would never be the same as it had been.

Fifty-six years later, Tommy would again deal with war. But this time, he would face it as Thomas Woodrow Wilson, twenty-eighth president of the United States.

FACTORY AND FARM

IN 1860 most of the nation's thirty-one million people lived in the country and worked as farmers. Families made their own clothing and many of the tools they needed.

There were differences, though, between the North and the South. The states of the North were home to nine out of ten U.S. factories. These factories used the latest technology to turn out modern machines and equipment for farms and homes. Trains moved these goods swiftly from factories to buyers.

The Southern states had few factories. Instead, there were many large farms called plantations. Southern planters raised vast amounts of cotton, tobacco, rice, and sugar. The planters relied on African American slaves to do all the backbreaking work. Without slaves to do the work, Southerners believed, there could be no cotton. And without cotton, the South's economy could not survive.

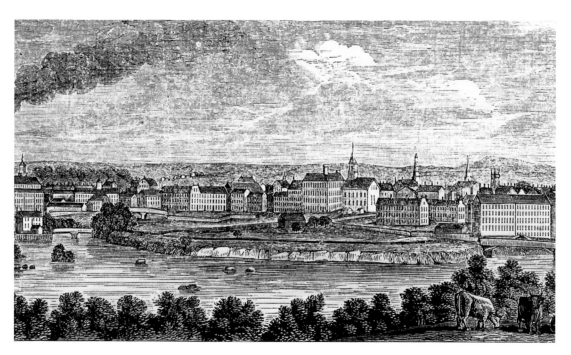

Cloth-making mills lined the river in the Northern manufacturing town of Lowell, Massachusetts.

THE COTTON GIN

A new invention, Eli Whitney's cotton engine, or "gin," could remove the seeds from cotton bolls far more rapidly than human hands. This meant that planters could harvest more cotton for a greater profit. Keeping up with the bigger harvest required thousands more slaves to work the fields. Because of the cotton gin, slave labor became even more important to the South.

"THE TUG HAS TO COME"

PEOPLE IN THE NORTH and those in the South strongly disagreed about slavery. Slavery was legal in the South, but Northerners had outlawed it in the early 1800s. People known as abolitionists struggled to abolish, or outlaw, slavery throughout the nation. Northern newspaperman William Lloyd Garrison and Sarah and Angelina Grimké—daughters of a Southern plantation owner— wrote newspaper articles and gave powerful speeches against slavery. Harriet Beecher Stowe's antislavery novel, *Uncle Tom's Cabin*, became famous across the country. Harriet Tubman, an escaped slave, helped other slaves escape to the North, with the aid of people living along the routes north. This network of people and secret routes to freedom was known as the Underground Railroad.

Then in 1860, a Northerner—Abraham Lincoln—was elected president of the United States. Voters knew that Lincoln was against slavery. Shortly after Lincoln's election, South Carolina seceded (withdrew) from the United States. President Lincoln was determined to preserve the United States as one nation. "Stand firm," Lincoln said to an advisor. "The tug [the pull to divide the nation] has to come."

Within months Mississippi, Alabama, and eight other states followed South Carolina's lead. They banded together to form the Confederate States of America, or the Confederacy, where slavery would remain legal. Early in 1861, the Confederacy elected Jefferson Davis its president.

Southern states began to secede from the United States soon after Abraham Lincoln *(above)* was elected president.

• • • •

"THERE IS A WAR COMMENCED"

THE UNITED STATES ARMY, called the Union Army, controlled four forts in the South. One of these was Fort Sumter in South Carolina. On April 12, 1861, the Confederates fired on the fort. The Northern soldiers inside the fort returned the gunfire. The battled raged for almost two days before the fort surrendered. The Civil War had begun.

Reports of Fort Sumter's fall jolted both the North and the South. Thirteen-year-old T. G. Barker was a student at a private school in South Carolina when he learned of the event:

> *We were in class all bent over our books, when Headmaster*
> *Hammond entered. . . . He went to the middle of the room and*

THE UNION AND THE CONFEDERACY

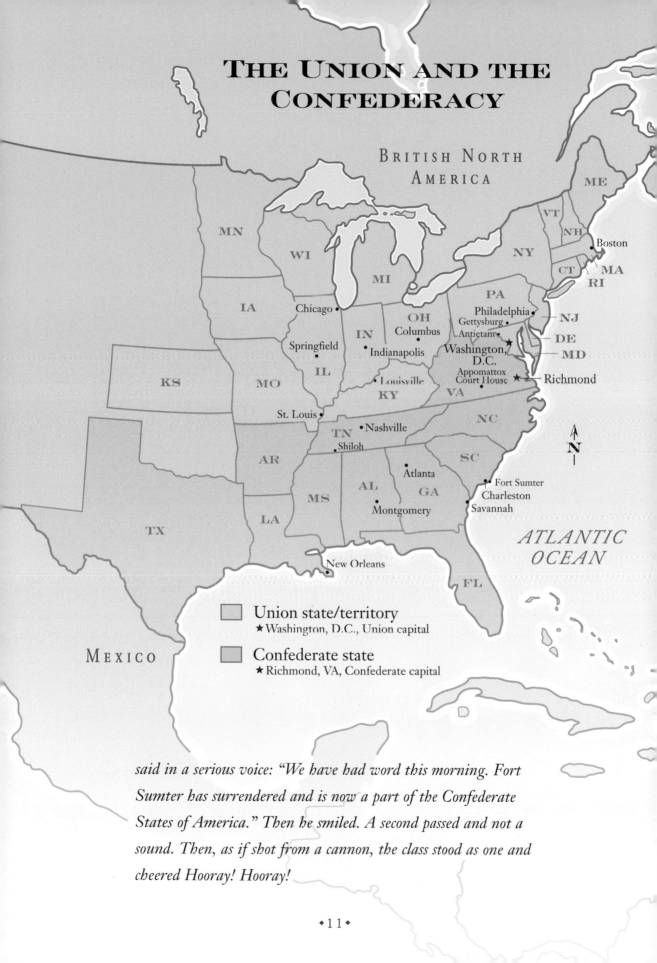

BRITISH NORTH
AMERICA

ME

MN

WI

MI

VT

NH

• Boston

NY

CT

MA

RI

IA

Chicago •

OH

PA

Philadelphia •

Gettysburg •

Antietam •

NJ

DE

IN

Columbus •

Springfield
•

• Indianapolis

Washington,
D.C.

★

MD

IL

• Louisville

Appomattox
Court House

★ — Richmond

KS

MO

KY

VA

St. Louis •

NC

TN

• Nashville

• Shiloh

SC

AR

Atlanta •

Fort Sumter

AL

GA

Charleston

MS

Montgomery •

Savannah

LA

TX

ATLANTIC
OCEAN

New Orleans •

FL

Union state/territory
★ Washington, D.C., Union capital

MEXICO

Confederate state
★ Richmond, VA, Confederate capital

N

said in a serious voice: "We have had word this morning. Fort
Sumter has surrendered and is now a part of the Confederate
States of America." Then he smiled. A second passed and not a
sound. Then, as if shot from a cannon, the class stood as one and
cheered Hooray! Hooray!

The War in Song and Verse

The North and the South used patriotic songs to inspire loyalty and confidence. "The Bonnie Blue Flag" was a Southern song that saluted the Confederate flag. The flag had red and white stripes and a single star in a blue triangle. James Sloan Gibbons, in the North, wrote the poem "We Are Coming, Father Abraham" in reaction to the news that Lincoln was drafting 300,000 men for the Union Army. Stephen Foster later set the poem to music.

The Bonnie Blue Flag

By Harry Macarthy

As long as the Union was faithful to her trust,
Like friends and like brothers we were kind, we were just;
But now when Northern treachery attempts our rights to mar,
We hoist on high the Bonnie Blue Flag that bears a single star.
Hurrah! Hurrah! for Southern Rights, hurrah!
Hurrah! for the Bonnie Blue Flag that bears a single star!

We Are Coming, Father Abraham

Words by James Sloan Gibbons
Music by Stephen Foster

We are coming, Father Abraham, three hundred thousand more,
From Mississippi's winding stream and from New England's shore;
We leave our plows and workshops, our wives and children dear,
With hearts too full for utterance, with but a single tear;
We dare not look behind us, but steadfastly before:
We are coming, Father Abraham, three hundred thousand more!

We are coming, we are coming, our Union to restore:
We are coming, Father Abraham, three hundred thousand more.
We are coming, Father Abraham, three hundred thousand more.

When fourteen-year-old Theodore Upson of Lima, Indiana, heard the news, he later remembered:

> Father and I were husking out some corn. . . . When William Cory came across the field he was excited and said, "Jonathan, the Rebels have fired and taken Fort Sumter." Father got white and couldn't say a word. William said, "The President will soon fix them. He has called for 75,000 men and is going to blockade their ports."

For African Americans living in the South, the shots fired at Fort Sumter had a different meaning. Hannah Crasson was an eight-year-old slave on a North Carolina plantation at the time. She recalled:

> My marster called my father and my two uncles, Handy and Hyman, our marster called them. . . . He said, "Come here and set down. I got something to tell you." [They] went to him and set down. He told them, "There is a war commenced between the North and the South. If the North whups [wins], you will be as free a man as I is. If the South whups, you will be a slave all your days."

After the attack on Fort Sumter in April 1861, President Lincoln immediately asked for 75,000 new troops. The South issued its own call to arms.

Enthusiasm ran high. Both sides were confident that their armies would quickly defeat the enemy. Hannah Crasson, the young North Carolina slave, recalled that when her master's son enlisted, "[He] said when he went to war that they could eat breakfast at home, go and whup the North and be back for dinner. He went away and it was four long years before he came back to dinner."

> "If the North whups [wins], you will be as free a man as I is. If the South whups, you will be a slave all your days."
>
> —Slave master of Hannah Crasson

Chapter Two

BUSY HANDS
AND
ANXIOUS
HEARTS

*"We children were in a constant state of
excitement; we were actors in the war."*

—Celine Fremaux, twelve, Baton Rouge, Louisiana, 1862

DURING THE 1860s, most Americans lived in extended families. For the seventeen million children aged sixteen or younger, family life generally meant lots of companions. A typical youngster of the time could expect brothers and sisters, aunts, uncles, grandparents, and maybe stepsiblings to be part of the household. A boarder who paid for a room and meals might also be on hand. New babies were welcomed as future helping hands. As they grew older, they would be able to do their share of work inside or outside the house.

Whether it was a town house, a farmhouse, or a two-room shack, the home was the center of family life. "A house," wrote one 1860s social observer, "is . . . the shell in which busy hands and anxious hearts combine their toil and hope."

Families looked to religion for comfort from the fear and losses caused by the war. "A . . . prayer meeting was held daily in the Presbyterian Chapel to pray for our Cause," recalled Annie Coulson, of Natchez, Mississippi. "It consoled our hearts to meet—united as we were by a common bond of sorrow."

Home could be a log cabin in a forest clearing *(opposite)*
or a comfortable house in town *(above)*.

FILLING THE LABOR GAP

IN A LETTER TO HER SOLDIER HUSBAND, Southerner Sarah
Kennedy told of changes
in their household. The
Kennedys' few slaves had
run off. Without her
husband or servants,
Sarah turned to her
children to fill the labor
gap. "Jimmy brings up
the coal and kindling
each evening," she wrote
to her husband proudly.
"He is my man of all
work. Sally minds the
little children. Mary goes
to school, but makes all
the beds every morning
before she leaves."

Even young children helped out at home when their
father left to fight the war.

The Kennedy family was not unusual. The war had taken young
and middle-aged men from their homes and farms. Often the women
and the children left at home had to take over the chores that had
been done by husbands and older sons. During the Civil War,
children made up the new workforce in the home.

TOWN AND COUNTRY

BEFORE DAYLIGHT, farm youngsters were out of bed and in the
barnyard. Boys might gather eggs that had been laid overnight and

feed the livestock. Milking the cows generally fell to the girls. One boy recalled that it was considered "too 'gal-ish' for a boy to milk."

Girls did the household cleaning, helped cook meals, learned to preserve fruits and vegetables, and even wove cloth. Boys chopped wood, groomed the horses, and fetched coal and kindling. The messy jobs of candle dipping and soap making were handled by both boys and girls. And with the war raging, older boys were often needed to help their mothers and grandfathers with plowing, planting, and harvesting.

Mornings were busy for city youngsters, too. There were stove fires to be stoked, water to be heated for cooking and washing, and breakfasts to make. One Pennsylvania boy living in a small town related, "Each day after the chamber work for the cows and horses was done [cleaning out the stable], I had to break the coal to be used for the next twenty-four hours. I was taught how to do everything around the house as well as mend my own clothing."

"I was taught how to do everything around the house as well as mend my own clothing."
—*A boy in Pennsylvania*

. . . .
THE NEW WORKPLACE

HUGE NUMBERS OF YOUNG PEOPLE labored outside the home, too. The laws of the 1860s allowed ten-year-olds to go to work. But children as young as six might work, too. With fathers off fighting, their families needed the extra money they could bring home.

More than 100,000 youngsters, in the North and in the South, worked in someone else's home as maids, servants, and stable boys.

THE FIRST FAMILIES

Being the son or daughter of a president did not guarantee happiness—or safety. Both First Families suffered tragic personal losses during the war.

Elizabeth Keckley, a free black, was Mrs. Lincoln's dressmaker and friend. This is her account of ten-year-old Willie Lincoln's fatal bout with "bilious fever" (probably typhoid):

His mother sat by his bedside a long while, holding his feverish hand in her own, and watching his labored breathing. . . . The night passed slowly; morning came and Willie was worse. He lingered a few days, and died. . . . I assisted in washing him and dressing him, and then laid him on the bed, when Mr. Lincoln came in. I never saw a man so bowed down with grief. He came to the bed, lifted the cover from the face of his child, gazed at it long and earnestly, murmuring, "My poor boy, he was too good for this earth. . . . It is hard, hard to have him die!" Great sobs choked his utterance. He buried his head in his hands, and his tall frame was convulsed with emotion.

Varina Howell Davis wrote an account of a family tragedy that occurred while her husband was the Confederate president:

> On April 30, 1864, when we were threatened on every side...Mr. Davis'[s] health had declined from loss of sleep so that he forgot to eat, and I resumed the practice of carrying him something at one o'clock. I left my children quite well, playing in my room, and had just uncovered my basket in his office, when a servant came for me. The most beautiful and brightest of my children, Joseph Emory, had, in play, climbed over the connecting angle of a bannister and fallen to the brick pavement below. He died a few minutes after we reached his side. This child was Mr. Davis'[s] hope, and greatest joy in life....A courier came with a dispatch. [Davis] took it, held it open for some moments....at last he tried to write an answer, and then called out, in a heartbroken tone, "I must have this day with my little child."

Opposite: Lincoln reads with his youngest son, Tad, whose brother Willie died during the Civil War. *Above:* In 1867 the surviving Davis children—Jeff Jr., Margaret, Varina Anne, and William—pose for a photograph after the end of the Civil War.

Giant mills and factories gradually became the main employer in the North. During the Civil War, 75,000 or more children labored in factories, mines, and mills. Child workers didn't have to worry about missing school. Most New England states, for example, required only fourteen weeks of school a year for young workers.

At least 75,000 children, mostly in the North, worked in factories, mines, and mills during the Civil War. These children are making twine in a New York City factory.

SCHOOLHOUSE BLUES

THE CIVIL WAR BROUGHT AN END to many children's education. Schools and colleges lost thousands of instructors and pupils to the war effort. In some cases, women substituted for male teachers, but many schools were forced to shut their doors. As early as October 1861, one teacher observed, "Students have all gone to war. College suspended, and God help the right."

"Students have all gone to war. College suspended, and God help the right."
—*A college teacher, 1861*

School closings were especially common in the South, where most of the war's battles were fought. In the early days of the war, many men, including teachers, eagerly volunteered for service. "I have the military fever very strong," one North Carolina teacher admitted. But the war dragged on and enthusiasm for fighting faded. Both North and South began to draft men, including teachers, to serve in the military.

Still, about one-half of the nation's twelve million school-age youth managed to attend classes of some kind. Free public education was available in the North. In the South, most youngsters were taught at home by their mothers or went to small local schoolhouses. Youth from wealthy families in both regions might attend expensive boarding schools either at home or in Europe.

Girls learned the art of embroidery in school, as well as reading, writing, and arithmetic.

Schoolhouses in rural areas were often one-room wooden buildings, cramped, poorly heated, and noisy. Students of all grades

PATRIOTIC PRIMER

Even in the classroom, war made itself felt. *Johnson's Elementary Arithmetic,* a North Carolina math primer (schoolbook), offered this problem:

> If one Confederate soldier can whip 7 Yankees [Northerners], how many soldiers can whip 49 Yankees?

were packed into a single classroom on hard plank benches. In some cases, there were no desks. Pupils had to write their lessons on slates, which were like small, crude chalkboards.

For most students, the war seemed to hover over home and school like rain clouds. Yet a lucky few were barely touched by it. "The war is raging," wrote sixteen-year-old Esther Alden of South Carolina in 1863. "But we, shut up here with our books and our little school tragedies and comedies, have remained very ignorant of all that is going on outside."

◆ ◆ ◆ ◆

"To Read above Anything Else"

SLAVES WHO ESCAPED TO FREEDOM were anxious to learn. Susie King, a young slave in Savannah, Georgia, had secretly learned to read as a child. When she was fourteen, she escaped with her uncle

For some young people, school shut out thoughts of the war.
For others, school gave them no relief.

Slaves in the South were not allowed to go to school. But they were eager to learn. Many former slaves, freed by Northern troops, went to Freedom Schools set up just for them.

and his family to one of Georgia's Sea Islands. Union troops had captured these islands off the coast. One of the Union officers asked Susie to teach the freed slaves on the island. She recalled, "I had about forty children to teach, besides a number of adults who came to me to read, to read above anything else."

At fifteen, Susie married a sergeant in the First South Carolina Colored Volunteers, a company of free black men. She lived with him at a camp at Port Royal, South Carolina. "I taught a great many of the comrades . . . to read and write when they were off duty. Nearly all were anxious to learn," she later wrote.

Chapter Three

SUNUP
TILL
SUNDOWN

"In a few hours the Yankees covered the town. . . . They told us we were all free."

—*Sarah Louise Augustus, eight, Fayetteville, North Carolina, 1865*

"COTTON IS KING," South Carolina senator James Hammond once declared, "and the African must be a slave." Most white Southerners agreed. Slavery made it possible for them to continue their way of life.

In the South, slaves were—first and last—white men's property. Slave owners believed they could more easily control workers who were ignorant. "We was not teached to read and write," recalled Patsy Mitchner, a former North Carolina slave. "You better not be caught with no paper in your hand. If you was, you got the cowhide [a whipping]." Slaves needed their owners' permission to marry or even visit friends at another plantation.

Opposite: Slaves picked cotton from sunup till sundown, then carried their full baskets to be weighed. *Above:* Even young people were sent to work in the fields.

◆ ◆ ◆ ◆

CHILDREN IN CHAINS

WILLIS COZART was fourteen years old when the Civil War broke out. He described life on his master's North Carolina plantation:

> It was a big plantation, 'round twelve hundred acres of land, I reckon. [My master] had about seventy or eighty slaves to work the cotton, corn, tobacco, and the wheat and vegetables. . . . The slave cabins was just log huts with sand floors, and stick-and-dirt chimneys. We was allowed to have a little patch of garden stuff at the back, but no chickens or pigs. The only way we had of

A group of newly escaped slaves rests at a farm in Maryland.

*making money was by picking berries and selling them. We ain't
had much time to do that, 'cause we worked from sunup till
sundown six days a week.*

The slave quarters, the area where the slaves lived, were usually
arranged in two long rows with a dirt street in between. Each family
lived in a cramped cabin of one or two rooms. "They had no floors,"
recalled Anne Maddox. "There wasn't no furniture 'cept a box for the
dresser with a piece of looking glass to look in." One small opening
served as a window.

Much of the food slaves ate was rationed by their masters. "Ever'
Sunday mo'nin' we all went to the Big House to get our week's supply
of food," Isom Norris reported. "We got plenty to last us until the next
Sunday, such as meat, flour, lard, peas, beans, potatoes and syrup."

Not every slave was this well fed. "We didn't have nuthin' to eat
through the week but cornbread and sweet 'taters," Jim Franklin
remembered.

"Too Small to Work"

A SLAVE'S LIFE on a plantation was endless work. For adults and teenagers, a day in a cotton or tobacco field meant eight to ten backbreaking hours of bending or stooping in the heat. They worked five and a half to six days a week. As Silas Jackson of Virginia remembered: "[You] were awakened by the blowing of the horn before sunrise by the overseer, started to work at sunrise and worked all day to sundown. . . . The slaves were driven at top speed and whipped at the snap of a finger by the overseers."

Younger children were usually spared the heaviest work. Isaac Johnson recalled, "They had me to do little things like feeding the chickens and minding the table sometimes; but I was too small to work. They didn't let children work much in them days till they were thirteen or fourteen years old." Other slave children began younger. Hannah Crasson was eight when the war began. "I swept yards, churned [made butter], fed the chickens," she reported. "In the evening, I would go with my missus a-fishing."

At outdoor slave markets across the South, white owners bought and sold slaves like cattle. Some slave owners were caring enough to avoid separating parents from children. Many were not. "I

Slaves were considered property. They were bought and sold without keeping families together. *Right:* A slave woman with her child begs not to be separated from her husband.

remembers the day we was put on the block [sold] in Richmond," Josephine Smith said. "I was just toddling around then, but me and my mammy brought $1,000. My daddy, I reckon, belonged to someone else. We was sold away from him just like the cow is sold away from the bull."

CONTRABANDS

President Lincoln freed the slaves in the Southern states during the war. But freedom didn't mean much to them until the Union Army took over Confederate areas in the South. Then many of the slaves left their masters and followed the Union soldiers *(below)*. At first, slaves who fled to the Union Army were treated as contraband (enemy property taken by an army). Later they were accepted as free men and women. Many found jobs with the military or lived in ragged camps near Union army camps.

Twelve-year-old Alex Huggins left his master in North Carolina. "Twasn't anythin' wrong about home that made me run away. I'd heard so much talk 'bout freedom, I reckon I jus' wanted to try it, and I thought I had to get away from home to have it," he recalled.

Yes, Mary I Sold You

Not all slaves were sold in public markets. Some sales took place right on the plantation. Such was the case with a young Texas slave named Mary Ferguson. Mary remembered:

About the middle of the evenin', up rode my young master on his hoss [horse], an' up drive two strange men in a buggy. They hitch their hosses an' come in the house, which scared me. Then one of the strangers said, "Git your clothes, Mary. We has bought you from Mr. Shorter." I commenced to cryin' an' beggin' Mr. Shorter not to let 'em take me away. But he said, "Yes, Mary, I sold you and you must go with them."

Us passed the very field where Paw an' all my folks was workin' an' I called out as loud as I could an' as long as I could see 'em "Good-bye, Ma! Good-bye, Ma!" But she never heard me. An' she couldn't see me, 'cause they had pushed me down out of sight on the floor of the buggy. I ain't never seed or heard tell of my Ma an' Paw, an' brothers an' sisters, from that day to this.

WHITE FRIEND, WHITE FOE

CHILDREN OF HOUSE SLAVES

(who worked in plantation mansions) had easier lives than children of field slaves. The white family might give an outgoing and imaginative slave child special privileges. White children often had a personal slave near their own age. The boys might climb trees, go fishing, catch frogs,

Sometimes a young slave was raised to be a companion to the master's child. Sometimes slave children were treated like a family pet.

pick berries, or roughhouse together. Master and slave daughters might play house, share dolls, or enjoy tea parties.

Betty Cofer recalled being a companion to her master's daughter:

> *I was lucky. Miss Ella was a little girl when I was borned, and she claimed me. We played together and grew up together. I waited on her and most times slept on the floor in her room. Ma was cook, and when I done got big enough, I helped to set the table in the big dining room. Then I'd put on a clean white apron and carry in the victuals [food] and stand behind Miss Ella's chair. She'd fix me a piece of something from her plate and hand it back over her shoulder to me.*

As the children grew older, this special relationship began to change. The companions became aware of the differences in their situations. In their games, the white boys and girls began to take charge. Slave children took their place as servants.

Chapter Four

The CHILDREN Are All SOLDIERS

"This was my birthday. I was ten years old, but I did not have a cake. Times were too hard so I celebrated with ironing."

—*Carrie Berry, ten, Atlanta, Georgia, 1864*

• •

IN WARTIME NEW CLOTHING was hard to find. For most ordinary people of the times, what they wore was designed to be practical. Men and boys who labored on the farm or in town wore clothes made from heavy, coarse fabrics to stand up to hard wear. Their jackets and pants were fashioned from denim or canvas. Shirts were most often made of cotton. Woolen vests could double for work or formal occasions. Suspenders, not belts, usually held up the trousers. Working-class men and boys sported straw hats or the popular broad-brimmed model.

Country and working-class women and girls wore long dresses of cotton or linsey-woolsey (a combination of linen and wool) that buttoned to the throat. Outdoors, they wore simple cotton bonnets that tied under the chin. Babies and toddlers of both sexes wore dresses that reached to their feet.

A farmboy went barefoot during the summer and often wore a straw hat.

DRESSING FOR THE SOCIAL SCENE

CLOTHING FOR WELL-TO-DO men and women reflected their place
in society. Professional men outfitted themselves in dark suits that fit loosely over white dress shirts and broad bow ties. Boys dressed like their fathers. Their jackets, however, were just waist-length and usually buttoned only near the top. In warm weather, boys wore short pants instead of long trousers until the boy reached his teens. With neatly cut hair, men wore tall silk or beaver fur hats. Young men sported soft cloth caps with short visors.

Fashionable town women wore large hoop-skirts. Their sons dressed like their fathers, but their jackets were shorter.

City women wore large hats decorated with feathers or flowers. Crinoline (linen and horsehair) petticoats or hoops (made of steel or whalebone) under the dress widened a woman's floor-length skirt. A lace-up garment called a corset reduced the size of her waist.

But there was a price to pay for looking fashionable. Hoopskirts were so wide that climbing into carriages or passing through doorways was a challenge. The wide bell shape of the skirts sometimes brought them dangerously close to fireplaces and stoves. Corsets often squeezed women's waists and ribs so snugly that they made it hard to move and to breathe.

Girls from wealthy families wore fashionable dresses much like their mothers', but mid-calf in length. Girls didn't have to wear tight corsets and awkward hoops. As they grew into their teens, girls work full, ankle-length dresses.

. . . .

FASHION AND WAR

THE WAR BROUGHT CHANGE to women's fashion, especially in the South. Before the war, the South had bought its cloth from the cloth-making mills of the North. Early in the war, President Lincoln ordered a naval blockade of the Southern coast. Patrolling Union ships kept Confederate and foreign ships from docking at Southern ports. The supply of cloth was cut off, and Southerners had to make do.

With a full set of hoops, a woman's skirt might require up to five yards of fabric. One way to save cloth was to make women's skirts smaller. New Orleans teenager Clara Solomon dealt with fabric shortages by resizing her hoops to make them "as diminutive [small]

GOOD ADVICE

Early rising and the habit of washing frequently in pure cold water are fine things for the health and complexion.

Physicians have agreed that it is better to keep the hair cut until the child is nine or ten years old. An abundance of hair at an early age is apt to produce weak eyes, paleness and head-ache.

Skating, driving hoops and other boyish sports may be practiced to great advantage by little girls, provided they can be pursued within the enclosure of a garden or court. In the street they would of course be improper.

–from *The Girl's Own Book* by Mrs. L. Maria Child, 1834

as possible." Many girls and women did away with hoops altogether. Cheaper, coarser fabrics soon showed up in both men's and women's garments, particularly underwear.

◆ ◆ ◆ ◆
FOOTWEAR

IN THE COUNTRY, hobnail shoes (with large-headed nails in the soles for walking on ice) were popular with men and women in winter. During the summer, young people often wore no shoes at all. When a boy finally reached the age when his feet stopped growing, he might receive his first pair of boots.

City men sported polished leather boots, often cut low at the top. Upper-class girls and women preferred high-topped leather or leather-and-fabric shoes that closed with hooks.

The war brought shortages of shoes as well. In 1863 seventeen-year-old Susan Bradford of Florida wrote, "I had no shoes except some terribly rough ones that old Mr. McDermid made. Cousin Rob tanned some squirrel skins and made me a pair of really beautiful shoes, nice enough to wear with my one and only silk dress."

"Cousin Rob tanned some squirrel skins and made me a pair of really beautiful shoes, nice enough to wear with my one and only silk dress."
—Susan Bradford, seventeen, Florida

Bertha Olmstead probably wore these satin slippers with a silk dress. The special occasion was her wedding on June 5, 1862, in Hartford, Connecticut.

HOLIDAYS AND SPECIAL DAYS

Children who lived during the Civil War often found holidays to be difficult times. The family of thirteen-year-old Celine Fremaux of Louisiana struggled to create cheer one Christmas. Their father, an engineer with the Southern army, was away fighting the war. Celine wrote:

We Fremaux children had never made much of Christmas. . . . Now this Christmas of 1863 we tried to celebrate. . . . It seemed so long since feast days, birthdays, or any notable occasion, that we anticipated some kind of joy. But all at once, when we gathered for the morning prayers we each and every one missed Father. And before we knew it Ma's voice was husky, and stopped, and we were all crying. Our little Christmas tree appeared some sort of sacrilege [not reflecting true devotion] to me. The day was spoiled, as every day was that we attempted to make gay, in those terrible years.

Southern slaves had even less to celebrate than whites. One of the more fortunate slave children was Eda Rains of Texas.

Our biggest time was at Christmas. Marster'd give us maybe fo' bits [four bits equals fifty cents, probably the total for the whole group of slave children] to spend as we wanted, and maybe we'd buy a string of beads or some such notion. On Christmas Eve, we played games:

"Young Gal Loves Candy" or "Hide and Whoop." Didn't know nothin' about Santa Claus, never was larned that. But we always knowed what we'd get on Christmas mornin'. Old Marster always call us together and give us new clothes—shoes, too. He always went to town on the Eve and brung us back our things in a cotton sack. That ol' sack'd be crammed full of things and we knowed it was clothes and shoes 'cause Marster didn't believe in no foolishness.

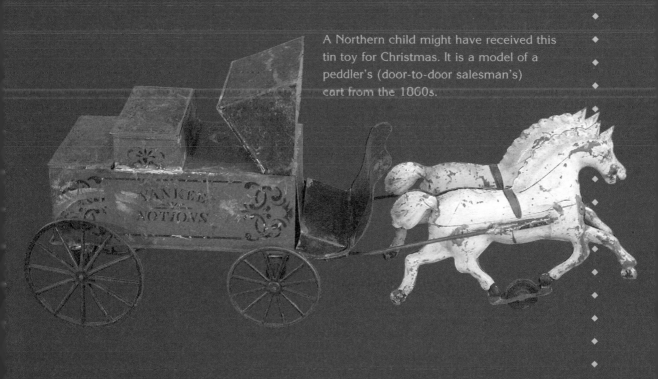

A Northern child might have received this tin toy for Christmas. It is a model of a peddler's (door-to-door salesman's) cart from the 1860s.

"BAREFOOTED AN' IN OUR SHIRTTAILS"

SLAVE CHILDREN usually received as
little clothing as possible. "Children
had only one piece, a long shirt,"
Alex Woods said of his childhood as a
slave. "We went barefooted an' in our
shirttails, we youngins did." Boys
were often teenagers before they got
their first pair of pants. For slave
girls, some cases were even more
extreme. "I went as naked as your
hand 'til I was fourteen years old,"
Mattie Curtis later told an
interviewer. "Marse Whitfield ain't
caring, but after that, Mammy told
him I had to have clothes."

These freed slaves were dressed in
tatters. Often, slave children
had few clothes.

THE DEVIL'S WORKSHOP

"IDLE HANDS ARE THE DEVIL'S WORKSHOP," ran a well-known
saying of the day. Yet youngsters who lived during the Civil War still
found leisure time and enjoyed it. Most children owned few store-
bought toys or games. Corncobs, wooden spoons, pots, lengths of
twine, and odd buttons might become dolls, dollhouses, puppets,
drums, play rifles, string toys, and tops.

Both girls and boys built pretend war camps and hospitals, drilled
and marched, and imitated admired generals. Fighting the war
became the new theme of the child's world of make-believe. One
woman wrote her husband, "The children are all soldiers here."

Outdoor activities were always popular. Children enjoyed skating and sledding during the winter. In warmer weather, boys swam in ponds and rivers, or played baseball. Dolls, dollhouses, and tea sets were the favorite toys of most girls, war or peace. Children of both sexes still played old-time games such as hide-and-seek, blind-man's buff, and marbles. For the well-to-do family, the new game of croquet became a favorite front lawn pastime.

Children enjoyed sledding wherever there was snow.

Reading remained one of the best-liked leisure activities. Popular authors of the day included Sir Walter Scott, Victor Hugo, and Wilkie Collins. Fiction and poetry provided a welcome escape for young people worried about the war. "Commenced reading 'Pilgrims of the Rhine,' am delighted with it!" Lucy Buck, eighteen, announced to her diary. "There seems to be so little real happiness that I would like to make for myself an imaginary life in the mimic [pretend] world created by the author's pen."

Young girls, North and South, played with dolls.

Chapter Five

OUR
SOLDIER
HEARTS

"Bullets flew thicker than bees and shells exploded with a deafening roar. I thought of home and friends, and how I would surely be killed, and how I didn't want to be!"

—Edward Spangler, sixteen, a Union soldier at the Battle of Antietam, 1862

◆ ◆

MOST PEOPLE followed the progress of the war closely. News of a victory, as Annie Coulson, twenty, said, "was as old wine to our soldier hearts." But whether battles were won or lost, there was always the worry about loved ones in combat. Ten-year-old Loulie Gilmer of Savannah wrote to her father telling him how much she missed him.

> *My Dear Dear Father,*
>
> *I do want to see you so much. I miss you so much in the evenings when I come in and no one is in, and I am so lonesome by myself[.] If you were here you would tell me stories and so I would not be so lonesome. I wish you would tell me one in your letter to me. . . . Auntie sends her love and hopes you are well and I hope so, too.*

Opposite: Families spent time together when a soldier had a brief leave. *Right:* Families also kept in touch through letters, sometimes written on patriotic stationery.

◆41◆

Southern women learned to make do as basic items grew scarce.
These women of the Confederacy gathered with their mending.

The Union naval blockade of Southern ports caused shortages that brought more hardship. Within months, families in the South began to feel the pinch. Basic items such as flour, coffee, pins, needles, matches, kettles, and linens grew scarcer. The shortage of coal and lamp oil meant that homes could not be heated or lit. Prices soared. In Richmond, Virginia, the weekly family food bill of $6.65 in 1861 rose to $68.25 by 1863. For families who still had money, this was a severe blow. Those who couldn't afford the higher prices made do, found substitutes, traded treasured belongings for food or cash, or did without.

Materials for uniforms, blankets, and bandages for Confederate troops also ran low. Southern women and children were quick to respond. Annie Coulson was part of the hometown war effort in Natchez, Mississippi. As she wrote:

> *The Court House and other public buildings were turned into sewing rooms, where the ladies daily gathered to sew for the soldiers. . . . Vast quantities of clothing were made in an astonishingly short time. The young girls were kept scraping lint*

[from old linen, to use in packing wounds] and rolling bandages to send with every box to the surgeon of each company. . . . Knitting socks was everybody's business. The children, both the boys and girls, were taught, and all the negro women.

◆ ◆ ◆ ◆

THE WAR COMES HOME

CELINE FREMAUX was twelve when Northern gunboats steamed up the Mississippi River to Baton Rouge, Louisiana, in August 1862. Within days, Northern troops were marching through the town. The firing began shortly afterward. Peering through a spyglass, Celine witnessed her first battle.

[I] saw guns aim, saw the sign to fire, saw men fall and rise, or try to rise, and fall again, never to move again. In one street, the Yankees seemed to be marching twelve or more abreast. The street

Union general William T. Sherman led his troops through Georgia, where the soldiers took their supplies from local plantations, often by force.

was packed. All at once a cannon back somewhere shot and shot again. . . . It mowed men down at a terrible rate. . . . It was blood, blood everywhere. I felt faint and I was sobbing.

Union soldiers also swarmed over Southern farms and plantations searching for food and horses. For the slaves, these raids could mean freedom. Sarah Louise Augustus was eight when Union troops arrived in her part of North Carolina.

They busted into the smokehouse at Marster's, took the meat, meal and other provisions. Grandmother pleaded with the Yankees, but it did no good. They took all they wanted. [Then] they told us we were all free. The Negroes begun visiting each other in the cabins, and became so excited they begun to shout and pray. I thought they were all crazy.

These boys and young men formed the drum corps of the 93rd New York Infantry.

"So I Became a Soldier"

Many teens and even some younger children caught the war fever. Southern boys wanted to defend their homeland from the Yankee invaders. Some young Northerners were dedicated to ending slavery. Some were fighting to reunite the Union. Many youngsters on both sides just wanted to escape the boredom of farm chores. To them the war seemed a grand adventure.

Military recruiters had instructions not to sign up any male under the age of eighteen. Younger boys lied about their age to get in. Thomas Galwey of Ohio had this experience: "I went to the armory of the [Irish American brigade]. They seemed to like me, and I liked them. So together with Jim Butler and Jim O'Reilly, I enlisted with them. I didn't tell them I was only fifteen. So I became a soldier."

Sixty thousand boys in the North and South took part in the war. They enlisted as drummers and buglers. Johnny Clem was eleven when he convinced the Twenty-Second Michigan Regiment to take him on as a drummer. In 1862 during the Battle of Shiloh in Tennessee, a stray shell fragment shattered his drum. The boy, however, was unhurt. This incident earned

Johnny Clem was eleven when he became a drummer for a Michigan regiment.

A call went out for African American men to join an all-black regiment from Massachusetts. Charles Miles Moore, fifteen, of Elmira, New York, rushed to volunteer. He became the drummer for Company H. Except for a brief period, Moore was with the regiment until the end of the war.

him the nickname Johnny Shiloh. Clem soon became a regular soldier and later earned the rank of sergeant.

African American slave boys were sometimes freed by the Union Army or escaped to find safety with Union troops. These freed slaves often became drummers, too. Some served Union officers or worked in camp kitchens.

Young men in military academies (schools) had a more direct route to the war. Seven of the eight military schools in the nation when the war broke out were in the South. One of these was the Virginia Military Institute. Beverly Stanard, eighteen, was enrolled. In May 1864, Stanard wrote his mother about his newest wartime adventure:

> *On Tuesday night an order came from General Breckinridge calling us immediately to Staunton [Virginia]. In obedience to his orders we fixed up and left on Wednesday morning at half past eight, marched 18 miles by half past two [o'clock], when we camped. . . . This morning we left camp under quite different circumstances, it having rained during the night and has continued all day. The roads were awful all the way and we had to wade through like hogs. . . . The Yankees are reported coming up the Valley with a force of 9,000 strong. I hope we may be able to lick them out. . . . You must not make yourself uneasy about me. I will take care of myself.*

THE REALITIES OF WAR

DREAMS OF GLORY and of easy victory faded quickly for youngsters in uniform. The routine of drilling and camp life was not exciting. Many recruits disliked gathering wood, hauling water, tending horses, cooking, and other daily duties. Even worse, army camps were filthy and filled with disease. Soldiers were twice as likely to die from an illness as from a wound.

The sight of the many badly wounded men gave young recruits a dose of reality. "It looked pretty tough to see the poor fellows—many of whom I knew—being taken back to the field hospital to be operated on," recalled Theodore Upson. "Once I . . . saw a pile of legs and arms as big as a haycock [haystack] where they were amputating. There were a great many stretched on the operating tables and the groans of the wounded were terrible."

William Bircher of Minnesota was a sixteen-year-old drummer when he first saw a battlefield. "Dead men were lying in the mud,

The war dead covered the ground after the battle of Gettysburg in Pennsylvania in 1863.

"WHERE ARE THE YANKEES?"

Alabama residents Emma Sansom, sixteen, and her mother saw a company of men wearing Union uniforms gallop past the house on May 2, 1863. Later, Confederate soldiers with a Yankee prisoner approached Emma and her mother. The Confederate officer said: "Ladies, do not be alarmed. I am General Forrest; I and my men will protect you from harm." Later, General Forrest asked Emma if she knew a way across the nearby creek. Emma recalled:

> I told him I knew of a trail about 200 yards above the bridge on our farm. . . . I believed he could get his men over there, and if he would have my saddle put on a horse I would show him the way. He said: "There is not time to saddle a horse; get up here behind me."

> We rode out into a field through which ran a [creek]. . . . Along there was a thick undergrowth that protected us from being seen by the Yankees at the bridge. . . . When we got to the creek, I said: "General Forrest, I think we had better get off the horse, as we are now where we may be seen."

> The cannon and other guns were firing fast by this time, as I pointed out to him where to go into the water and out on the other bank. . . . He asked me my name and asked me to give him a lock of my hair.

The next day, Forrest's troops surprised and captured the entire Union force—thanks in part to Emma's help.

mixed up with sacks of grain and government stores [supplies]," he recalled. "Some [were] lying in the water and others trampled entirely out of sight in the deep mud."

But the ultimate experience of the war was being under enemy fire. Thomas Galwey described the terrible losses suffered by his unit from Confederate bombardment:

> *Lieutenant Delany is shot. . . Lieutenant Lantry, poor fellow, is annihilated [killed] instantly, near me. The top of his head is taken off by a shell . . . . There is but a small group of us left. Fairchild is bleeding; Campion falls, mortally wounded; Jim Gallegher's head is badly grazed and he rolls, coiled in a lump, down into a ditch.*

Elisha Stockwell of Wisconsin had run away from home to enlist in 1861. A year later, the sixteen-year-old found himself pinned down by Confederate fire near the small Tennessee church called Shiloh. Elisha and his comrades had just been stirring from sleep when Confederate troops attacked. "As we lay there and the shells were flying over us, my thoughts went back to my home," he later wrote. "I thought what a foolish boy I was to run away to get into such a mess as I was in. I would've been glad to see my father coming after me."

> *"As we lay there and the shells were flying over us, my thoughts went back to my home."*
> —Elisha Stockwell, sixteen

Stockwell, Thomas Galwey, and Theodore Upson were three of the lucky ones. They survived not only individual battles, but the war as well. Others were not so fortunate. Three days after writing his May 1864 letter to his mother, Beverly Stanard was killed in action near New Market, Virginia.

Chapter Six

NEW FRONTIERS

"How dreadfully sick I am of this war. . . . It commenced when I was thirteen, and I am now seventeen, and no prospect of its ending."

—Emma Le Conte, *seventeen, Columbia, South Carolina, 1865*

FOUR LONG YEARS of fighting on Civil War battlefields brought death and destruction to millions of Americans. The four years of conflict seemed an eternity to Emma Le Conte and to many other young people. Yet life went on—if not quite normally. Infants grew into toddlers. Young children became teenagers. Teens matured to early adulthood. Young people went through the phases and changes of the growing-up process.

The most obvious changes occurred during the teen years. As hormones shifted and flowed, boys and girls could see and feel their bodies developing. Skin problems were common. But even treating acne could be risky. One popular acne remedy, Fowler's Solution, contained the deadly poison arsenic.

◆ ◆ ◆ ◆

MAKING THEIR WAY

BY THEIR EARLY TEENS, young people were already thinking about the future. In choosing their life's work, boys might have many choices. A son entered his father's trade or business. Or his father might arrange for him to be apprenticed to a carpenter, bricklayer, or other skilled workman. There he would train for a number of years to learn the trade.

Opposite: Home at last! *Right:* Girls grew into young ladies as the war dragged on.

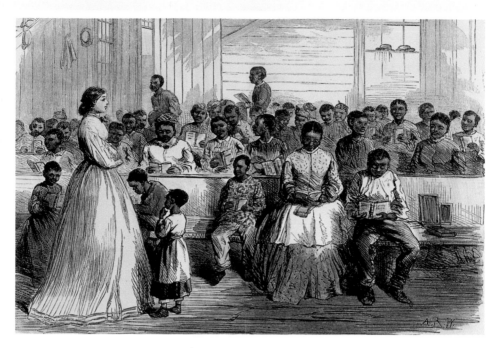

Women often worked as teachers, and some taught at
Freedom Schools *(above)* for former slaves.

Sometimes a young man wanted to be a lawyer, minister, or
banker. He needed money and education to get into those
professions. Attending a university brought a young man friendships
that could help his career.

Women had fewer career choices. Many professions and trades
were not considered suitable for women. Most girls looked forward
to happiness as wives and mothers. It was not unusual, however, for
women to work as teachers, governesses, or household servants.
Some worked in the mills. Others became dressmakers, hatmakers,
and shopkeepers.

The war both decreased and increased job opportunities. The
conflict destroyed cities, factories, and businesses in the South.
Factories in the North and the South lost male employees who left
to fight the war. So girls and women took their places. On the other
hand, the war created careers for older boys and men in both the

Union and Confederate armies. Some recruits planned to stay in the military after the war—if they lived through it.

• • • •

"THIS HUNGER OF THE HEART"

OF COURSE, there were other, gentler matters to think about, too. Growing up was just as important in the 1860s as it is in modern times. On September 25, 1862, Lucy Buck wrote about her emotions in her diary: "My birthday! Twenty years old! . . . I *am* a woman in *feelings* as well as *years*. A woman by this passionate longing and yearning—this hunger of the heart."

Not surprisingly, the war added new drama to romantic relationships. In the South and the North, patriotic feelings ran as warmly in females as in males. To many young women, a man in uniform showed courage and loyalty to the North or to the South. Young men took notice. "If a fellow wants to go with a girl now he had better enlist," Theodore Upson observed. "The girls sing 'I Am Bound to Be a Soldier's Wife or Die an Old Maid'."

Like many young men, Upson made the most of it. "I had rather liked E. S.[a young woman] for a long time [but] never could muster up courage enough to ask her to go any place with me."

Military men impressed young women.

Once Theodore enlisted, the same young lady began to notice him. He found the nerve to ask her to a picnic. "We had a fine time at the picnic. E. S. and I went in a buggy together. I had never taken a girl in that way before and felt a little shy and green but liked it ever so much. . . . She has given me her picture and promised to write me after I am gone."

> *"She has given me her picture and promised to write me after I am gone."*
>
> —Theodore Upson,
> Indiana enlisted man

A young man interested in a young woman would call on her at home. The girl's parents and even her brothers and sisters were often present. The evening would be spent in polite conversation, parlor games, or some musical activity. As the romance warmed up, the young man would escort the girl to parties, dances, and other get-togethers. He might also accompany her and her family to church.

If the couple decided on marriage, the young man usually followed the custom of asking the girl's parents for her hand. It was a happy, yet sobering time. The leap into marriage was both exciting and serious. For many, it was the final step into adulthood.

◆ ◆ ◆ ◆

THE WAR ENDS

BY THE SPRING of 1865, the South could hold out no longer. Confederate general Robert E. Lee surrendered his army to Union general Ulysses S. Grant on April 9 at Appomattox Court House, Virginia. At home in Front Royal, Virginia, Lucy Buck heard the news on April 13:

> *Father came in suddenly pale and grave with the words "Well, I fear the die is cast—Lee has surrendered"—almost torn from his*

lips. If the heavens had fallen there could scarcely have been
greater [distress] and grief in our midst. . . . Our dearest hopes
dashed—our fondest dreams [gone]—we and our brave ones who
had struggled, bled and suffered—slaves and to such a tyrant.

Wisconsin teen soldier Elisha Stockwell and his Union comrades were stationed outside of Montgomery, Alabama. They received word of Lee's surrender there. Stockwell wrote:

We got news that General Lee had surrendered, and we lay
there all day and celebrated. They lined up the [weapons] of the
whole command and fired a gun just about as fast as one could
count. An officer sat on a horse at the right of the gun, and he
had a small flag called a guidon. Every time he made a motion
down a gun was fired. So the firing was as regular as a clock.
This sounded nice to us as it was the [end] of secession, and
meant the cruel war was over.

General Robert E. Lee *(seated, center)* surrenders to
Union general Ulysses S. Grant *(seated, right)*.

After the war, the South struggled to rebuild burned-out farms, towns, and cities such as Richmond, Virginia *(above)*.

Three days after Lee's surrender, President Lincoln was murdered at Ford's Theatre in Washington, D.C., by actor John Wilkes Booth. The North mourned its dead leader. Samuel Gompers, a teenaged immigrant worker and future labor leader, was in New York at the time of Lincoln's death. He wrote:

> *I remember very vividly the morning that brought the news of President Lincoln's death. . . . It seemed to me that some great power for good had gone out of the world. A master mind had been taken at a time when most needed.*

Families in the North and in the South struggled to carry on. A staggering 620,000 men had died during the war, and 420,000 returned home wounded or crippled. North and South had suffered heartbreaking losses of family members, neighbors, and friends. The South had also witnessed the terror of invading armies. They had seen the burning of homes, public buildings, fields, and farms.

Celine Fremaux had moved with her family to Jackson, Louisiana, to avoid the fighting. But there was no escaping its outcome or what happened afterward.

> The War was done. But what next? We were not hearing from Father or Leon [her brother]. Then the soldiers began to come home. . . . Coming home where no home remained. Many never found their families. Many were years finding them.

Young sergeant Theodore Upson saw the end of the war this way:

> Of the thousand officers and men who started out with us, 474 were not with us now. Many had met death on Southern battlefields; some in hospitals far from home and friends had given all they had to give—their lives. . . . But from those who have lived to return come no words of regret. . . . What we went out to do is done. The war is ended, and the Union is saved!

Black Union troops, leaving the army in Little Rock, Arkansas, are greeted by their loved ones.

ACTIVITIES

STUDY HISTORICAL ILLUSTRATIONS

What can we learn from studying old photographs?

This photo was taken in 1862 on a farm in Maryland. It shows people newly escaped from slavery. Study the larger image on page 26 for a moment. Look carefully at the setting, the people, and the details of the picture. After you've used your eyes and brain to collect information, let your imagination take over.

With disposable or digital cameras, we can snap pictures of family or friends anytime. But how easy was photography in Civil War times? Note the positions and expressions of the people in the photos. Do they look cheerful or serious? Hopeful for the future? Does the group appear natural or do they seem carefully posed?

Taking a photograph was a complicated process in 1862. It was easier to keep a serious expression than a smile during the long exposure time. The child sitting in the front row couldn't keep still that long, so his head is a blur.

It's clear that everyone in this photo was born into slavery. (Remember, the date of the picture is 1862.) They can look forward to a future free of slavery. Most of the adults seem fairly young. They and their children will have many free years ahead of them. Some may go north or west, looking for new opportunities. Some may return to farming in the South, even working for hire on the plantation where they were slaves. Are they hopeful for their futures, eager to learn and work and raise their families, unafraid of forced separation? Or might they see the problems and struggles, brought about by the new freedom, and worry about what lies ahead?

We'll probably never know the answers to these questions. But isn't it interesting to guide our imaginations through the ideas inspired by this picture?

Play a Game from Civil War Times

Ring-Taw* (*A game of marbles; a* taw *is a large, fancy marble used for shooting*)

Players draw a circle on the ground. Each player places an agreed-upon number of marbles inside this ring. Players then draw a line, called the offing, at some distance from the circle. From there each person takes a turn to shoot a taw at the ring. The goal is to strike others' marbles out of the ring. If successful, the player gets to shoot the taw again from where it landed. (A good player may clear the circle before anyone else gets a chance to shoot.) The player also wins each marble struck from the circle.

After the first round, each player shoots from the place their taw came to rest on the previous round. If a taw remains in the circle, that player is out of the game, and all marbles previously won from opponents must be returned to the ring. The player whose taw is struck by another's taw is also out and must give all marbles won to the player with the striking taw. The game ends when only one taw remains in action.

Cook Civil War Style

Johnnycakes

Ingredients

1 cup water

1½ cups ground yellow cornmeal

½ teaspoon salt

½ cup milk

2 tablespoons butter

molasses or maple syrup and butter

Equipment

small saucepan

liquid measuring cup

large mixing bowl

dry measuring cups

measuring spoons

wooden spoon for serving

large skillet

spatula

Directions

1. Bring 1 cup water to boil in saucepan.

2. Combine the boiling water with 1½ cups cornmeal, ½ teaspoon salt, and ½ cup milk in bowl. Stir well.

3. Melt 2 tablespoons butter in skillet over medium heat.

4. Pour 1 tablespoon of batter for each cake into skillet. Cook over medium heat 4 to 5 minutes on each side. Cook until edges are lacy and lightly browned. Turn gently with spatula and cook for another minute.

5. Serve hot with molasses, or with maple syrup and butter.

Source Notes

7 Lucy R. Buck, *Shadows on My Heart: The Civil War Diary of Lucy Rebecca Buck of Virginia*, ed. Elizabeth Baer (Athens, GA: University of Georgia Press, 1997), 4.

7 Woodrow Wilson, quoted in Ray Stannard Baker, ed., *Woodrow Wilson: Life and Letters—Youth, 1856–1890* (New York: Greenwood Press, 1968), 28.

10 Abraham Lincoln, quoted in Geoffrey Ward, *The Civil War: An Illustrated History* (New York: Alfred A. Knopf, 1990), 26.

10–11 T. G. Barker, quoted in Jim Murphy, *The Boys' War* (New York: Clarion, 1990), 6.

12 Harry Macarthy, "The Bonnie Blue Flag," in Lois Hill, ed., *Poems and Songs of the Civil War* (New York: The Fairfax Press, 1990), 210.

12 James Sloan Gibbons, "We Are Coming, Father Abraham," in Hill, 213–214.

13 Theodore F. Upson, *With Sherman to the Sea*, ed. Oscar Osburn Winther (Bloomington, IN: Indiana University Press, 1958), 9–10.

13 Hannah Crasson, quoted in Belinda Hurmence, ed., *My Folks Don't Want Me to Talk about Slavery: Twenty-One Oral Histories of Former North Carolina Slaves* (Winston-Salem, NC: John F. Blair, 1984), 19–20.

14 Celine Fremaux Garcia, *Celine: Remembering Louisiana, 1850–1871*, ed. Patrick J. Geary (Athens, GA: University of Georgia Press, 1987), 74.

15 Daniel E. Sutherland, *The Expansion of Everyday Life: 1860–1876* (New York: Harper & Row, 1990), 52.

15 Annie Harper Coulson, *Annie Harper's Journal: A Southern Mother's Legacy*, ed. Jeannie M. Deen (Corinth, MS: The General Store, 1983), 12.

16 Sarah Kennedy, quoted in Drew Gilpin Faust, *Mothers of Invention: Women of the Slaveholding South in the American Civil War* (Chapel Hill: University of North Carolina Press, 1996), 130.

17 James Reger, *Life in the South during the Civil War* (San Diego, CA: Lucent Books, 1997), 61–62.

17 Sutherland, 54–55.

18 Elizabeth Keckley, *Behind the Scenes, or Thirty Years a Slave and Four Years in the White House* (New York: Oxford University Press, 1988), 23–24.

19 Varina Howell Davis, quoted in Katharine M. Jones, ed., *Heroines of Dixie*, Vol. II (Marietta, GA: Mockingbird Books, 1955), 82.

20 Ibid., 26.

20 Maury Klein, *Life in Civil War America* (Jamestown, VA: Eastern Acorn Press, 1987), 26.

21 Ibid., 27.

22 Esther Alden, quoted in Jones, 21.

23 Susie King Taylor, *Reminiscences of My Life in Camp* (New York: Arno Press and the New York Times, 1968), 11.

24 Sarah Augustus, quoted in Hurmence, 27.

25 James Hammond, quoted in Ward, 12.

25 Patsy Mitchner, quoted in Hurmence, 77.

25–26 Willis Cozart, quoted in Hurmence, 89.

26 Anne Maddox, quoted in Donna Wyant Howell, ed., *I Was a Slave*, Book 5, *The Lives of Slave Children* (Washington, D.C.: American Legacy Books, 1997), 11.

26 Isom Norris, quoted in Howell, 12.

26 Jim Franklin, Ibid., 14.

27 Silas Jackson, Ibid., 31.

27 Isaac Johnson, quoted in Hurmence, 21.

27 Hannah Crasson, quoted in Howell, 19.

28 Josephine Smith, Ibid., 32.

28 Alex Huggins, quoted in Emmy E. Werner, *Reluctant Witnesses: Children's Voices from the Civil War* (Boulder, CO: Westview Press, 1988), 40.

29 Mary Ferguson, quoted in Reger, 55.

30 Betty Cofer, quoted in Howell, 68.

32 Carrie Berry, quoted in Phillip Hoose, *We Were There, Too!: Young People in U.S. History* (New York: Farrar Strauss & Giroux, 2001), 121.

34 Mrs. L. Maria Child, *The Girl's Own Book* (1834. Reprint, Bedford, MA: Applewood Books [in cooperation with Old Sturbridge Village],1992), 281, 283.

34–35 Clara Solmon, quoted in Faust, 225.

35 Susan Bradford, quoted in Jones, 49.

36 Fremaux Garcia, 123–124.

36–37 Eda Rains, quoted in Hurmence, 7.

38 Alex Woods, quoted in Howell, 22.

38 Mattie Curtis, quoted in Hurmence, 36.

38 Ellen Moore, quoted in Faust, 130.

39 Lucy Buck, quoted in Baer, 41.

41 Edward Spangler, quoted in Werner, 30–31.

41 Coulson, 11.

41 Loulie Gilmer, quoted in Jones, *Heroines of Dixie:* Vol. I, 100–101.

42–43 Coulson, 11.

43–44 Fremaux Garcia, 82–84.

44 Sarah Augustus, quoted in Hurmence, 27.

45 Thomas Galwey, quoted in Murphy, 11.

46 Beverly Stanard, *Letters of a New Market Cadet*, ed. John Barrett and Robert Turner (Chapel Hill, NC: University of North Carolina Press, 1961), 61.

47 Upson, 86.

48 Emma Sansom, quoted in Jones, *Heroines of Dixie:* Vol. I, 228–231.

49 William Bircher, quoted in Werner, 25.

49 Thomas Galwey, quoted in Murphy, 70.

49 Elisha Stockwell, Ibid., 33.

50 Emma Le Conte, quoted in Werner, 127.

53 Buck, 152.

53 Upson, 19.

53–54 Ibid.,19–20.

54–55 Buck, 319.

55 Elisha Stockwell, quoted in Murphy, 91–92.

56 Samuel Gompers, *Seventy Years of Life and Labor:* Vol. I (New York: E. P. Dutton, 1925), 27.

57 Fremaux Garcia, 148–149.

57 Upson, 181.

59 William Clarke, *The Boy's Own Book* (1829. Reprint. Bedford, MA: Applewood Books [in cooperation with Old Sturbridge Village], 1996), 11.

Selected Bibliography

Baker, Ray Stannard, ed. *Woodrow Wilson: Life and Letters—Youth, 1856–1890.* New York: Greenwood Press, 1968.

Biel, Timothy Levi. *Life in the North during the Civil War.* San Diego, CA: Lucent Books, Inc., 1997.

Buck, Lucy R. *Shadows on My Heart: The Civil War Diary of Lucy Rebecca Buck of Virginia.* Edited by Elizabeth Baer. Athens, GA: University of Georgia Press, 1997.

Catton, Bruce. *The Civil War.* New York: Fairfax Press, 1980.

Child, Mrs. L. Maria. *The Girl's Own Book.* 1834. Reprint, Bedford, MA: Applewood Books (in cooperation with Old Sturbridge Village), 1992.

Clarke, William. *The Boy's Own Book.* 1829. Reprint, Bedford, MA: Applewood Books (in cooperation with Old Sturbridge Village), 1996.

Coulson, Annie Harper. *Annie Harper's Journal: A Southern Mother's Legacy.* Edited by Jeannie M. Deen. Corinth, MS: The General Store, 1983.

Dosier, Susan. *Civil War Cooking: The Union.* Mankato, MN: Blue Earth Books, 2000.

Faust, Drew Gilpin. *Mothers of Invention: Women of the Slaveholding South in the American Civil War.* Chapel Hill, NC: University of North Carolina Press, 1996.

Garcia, Celine Fremaux. *Celine: Remembering Louisiana, 1850–1871.* Edited by Patrick J. Geary. Athens, GA: University of Georgia Press, 1987.

Gompers, Samuel. *Seventy Years of Life and Labor.* Vol. I. New York: E. P. Dutton, 1925.

Greene, Meg. *Slave Young, Slave Long.* Minneapolis: Lerner Publications Company, 1999.

Hill, Lois, ed. *Poems and Songs of the Civil War.* New York: The Fairfax Press, 1990.

Holzer, Harold. *Witness to War: The Civil War.* New York: Berkley Publishing Group, 1996.

Hoose, Phillip. *We Were There, Too!: Young People in U.S. History.* New York: Farrar Strauss & Giroux, 2001.

Howell, Donna Wyant, ed. *I Was a Slave.* Book 5, *The Lives of Slave Children.* Washington, D.C.: American Legacy Books, 1997.

Hurmence, Belinda, ed. *My Folks Don't Want Me to Talk about Slavery: Twenty-One Oral Histories of Former North Carolina Slaves.* Winston-Salem, NC: John F. Blair, 1984.

Jones, Katharine M., ed. *Heroines of Dixie.* 2 vols. Marietta, GA: Mockingbird Books, 1955.

Keckley, Elizabeth. *Behind the Scenes, or Thirty Years a Slave and Four Years in the White House.* New York: Oxford University Press, 1988.

Klein, Maury. *Life in Civil War America.* Jamestown, VA: Eastern Acorn Press, 1987.

Leisch, Juanita. *An Introduction to Civil War Civilians.* Gettysburg, PA: Thomas Publications, 1994.

Murphy, Jim. *The Boys' War.* New York: Clarion Books, 1990.

Reger, James. *Life in the South during the Civil War.* San Diego, CA: Lucent Books, 1997.

Stanard, Beverly. *Letters of a New Market Cadet.* Edited by John Barrett and Robert Turner. Chapel Hill, NC: University of North Carolina Press, 1961.

Sutherland, Daniel E. *The Expansion of Everyday Life: 1860–1876.* New York: Harper & Row, 1990.

Taylor, Susie King. *Reminiscences of My Life in Camp.* New York: Arno Press and the New York Times, 1968.

Upson, Theodore F. *With Sherman to the Sea.* Edited by Oscar Osburn Winther. Bloomington, IN: Indiana University Press, 1958.

Ward, Geoffrey. *The Civil War: An Illustrated History.* New York: Alfred A. Knopf, 1990.

Werner, Emmy E. *Reluctant Witnesses: Children's Voices from the Civil War.* Boulder, CO: Westview Press, 1988.

Wisler, G. Clifton. *When Johnny Went Marching: Young Americans Fight the Civil War.* New York: HarperCollins, 2001.

FURTHER READING

Arnold, James R., and Roberta Wiener. *Divided in Two: The Road to Civil War, 1861*. Minneapolis: Lerner Publications Company, 2002.

———. *Life Goes On: The Civil War at Home, 1861–1865*. Minneapolis: Lerner Publications Company, 2002.

———. *Lost Cause: The End of the Civil War, 1864–1865*. Minneapolis: Lerner Publications Company, 2002.

———. *On to Richmond: The Civil War in the East, 1861–1862*. Minneapolis: Lerner Publications Company, 2002.

———. *River to Victory: The Civil War in the East, 1861–1863*. Minneapolis: Lerner Publications Company, 2002.

———. *This Unhappy Country: The Turn of the Civil War, 1863*. Minneapolis: Lerner Publications Company, 2002.

Bial, Raymond. *The Strength of These Arms: Life in the Slave Quarters*. Boston: Houghton Mifflin, 1997.

Bolotin, Norman, and Angela Herb. *For Home and Country: A Civil War Scrapbook*. New York: Lodestar Books, 1995.

Catton, Bruce. *The Civil War*. New York: Fairfax Press, 1980.

Chang, Ina. *A Separate Battle: Women and the Civil War*. New York: Lodestar Books, 1991.

Channing, Steven A. *Confederate Ordeal: The Southern Home Front*. Alexandria, VA: Time-Life Books, 1984.

Currie, Stephen. *Life of a Slave on a Southern Plantation*. San Diego, CA: Lucent Books, 2000.

Damon, Duane. *When This Cruel War Is Over: The Civil War Home Front*. Minneapolis: Lerner Publications Company, 1996.

Day, Nancy. *Your Travel Guide to Civil War America*. Minneapolis: Runestone Press, 2001.

Jackson, Donald Dale. *Twenty Million Yankees: The Northern Home Front*. Alexandria, VA: Time-Life Books, 1985.

Ray, Delia. *Behind the Blue and Gray: The Soldier's Life in the Civil War*. New York: Lodestar Books, 1991.

INDEX